My Mom Works in the School Lunchroom

Titus Schorr

Rosen REAL READERS

Rosen Classroom™
New York

My mom works at a school.

She works in
the school lunchroom.

My mom washes food.

My mom cuts food.

My mom cooks food.

My mom gives food
to students.

Words To Know

to cook

to cut

lunchroom

to wash